Film is un-dead!

*Why you should get (back) into film
photography and how to truly enjoy the
analog experience.*

DENNIS EIGHTEEN

DEDICATION

For Julia

CONTENTS

Open shutter!

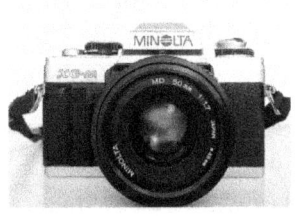

So did film die? Yes, it did. However, you will find that film is still around. Film as well as analog cameras are best described as un-dead, rather than dead.

„Film is un-dead" blatantly promotes getting (back) into analog photography and gives tips and advice on how to discover an entirely unique world filled with magic and wonder. Of course it also talks about technical aspects of shooting with film. If you stop reading now, let me say this: Shoot film! It's fun. It makes you a better photographer and you will make more friends than you can handle. If you do not want to stop reading: Thanks and please turn the page!

Why should anyone even think about using film?

Everyone talks about digital this and digital that. The conversations between photographers or between photographer and camera salesperson, for that matter, revolve around megapixels, ISO performance and the resolution of the LCD screen on the back of the body or the EVF (electronic view finder). If you look at photography magazines, it's all about the newest, shiniest electronic gadget that will make you the best photographer in the world. Turn on your tablet, desktop computer or Smartphone, go to YouTube and you will find an army of people holding up the coolest DSLR, mirrorless or compact cameras on the market. Amateur youtubers and professionals alike talk through the menus and sub-menus. They pontificate on sensor size and battery life, not to mention the maximum number of frames-per-second, HDR, low-pass filters (whatever the heck that is!) and the 1080p HD or 4K video capability of the wonderful camera they are trying to sell you.

From all of this, one can get the impression that film is indeed dead. If you go to a camera store and ask for film you may be led to a shelf in the back of the store and be sold a few rolls like contraband from the trunk of a car. Asking the kid behind the counter at your local drugstore for film will get you the most puzzled look a teenager is capable of.

So did film die? Yes, it did. However, you will find that film is still around. Film, as well as analog cameras, are best described as un-dead, rather than dead.

If you look closely you will find that in the shadows there is an army of enthusiastic film shooters. Professionals and hobbyists alike keep the art and craft of analog photography from dying completely—and they're doing a great job. First and foremost they are creating great photos. Their pictures are seen on billboards, ads, galleries, books, and all over the Internet. Once you start looking, you'll realize analog shooters are everywhere. Like the good vampires, they walk the earth with grace, are pretty darn sexy and don't really care about hype and current trends, for their magic has been around for ages and will never disappear.

Let's leave the un-dead metaphor and talk about why you should consider shooting film again—or maybe for the first time.

First of all, it really is fun! Nothing beats the feeling you get when you hear the sound of the shutter and film advance. Nothing creates a bigger sensation of longing than the wait for the pictures to come back from the lab. And very little in the world tops the joy and excitement you experience when you open up that pack of prints or if you load that CD into your computer and see the moments you have captured for all eternity.

Second, shooting film makes you a better photographer. Having all the important aspects of taking a photograph at your fingertips gives you the ultimate control of the end product. No software or processor makes the decisions—you do! Doing things manually along with the limitations of the number of frames per roll of film forces you to think. Film shooters work slower than their digital friends. „Spray and pray" is not a viable option for someone shooting film. The analog photographer wants to make every frame count, unless they are Lomographers, but we will discuss that later.

Thirdly, shooting film lets you make new friends. When is the last time you stopped a guy on the street lugging around a DSLR and asked him about his camera? My best guess is: never. You just don't stop Joe Digital and ask him about his gear—unless you are desperately in need of a friend and don't really care about the camera. However , in the past couple of years, if you have been out and about shooting with an analog „Fotoapparat," you will almost certainly have experienced curious questions from strangers. The most common: „Can you still get film for that?" Usually that question is accompanied by acclamations as to the awesomeness of the apparatus and your personal coolness and genius for being able to work one of these things. If you are single—let this be the plug for the yet to be written bestselling book „How to find the love of your life"— then you should consider getting a Polaroid camera.

Those things are the ultimate conversation starters and you always have a little present to write your phone number on.

If you have not guessed by this point, this book is a labor of love. I have written it because I firmly believe in the magic of analog photography and want everyone— and especially you, dear reader—to pick up an analog camera, buy a roll of film and go make photographs! I say MAKE, because that is what you do. Digital photographers TAKE photos. Analog photographers MAKE them.

I am not saying that analog photography is better than digital. That is a war of religion and nothing ever good comes out of one of those. Both have their place and both roads can lead to Photo-Nirvana. No doubt, there are great artists around who create stunning images with purely digital equipment. I would recommend, you check out: Zack Arias, Chase Jarvis and Jeremy Cowart. Seriously, go check them out! You will start looking for the Arias-, Jarvis- or Cowart-"button" on your camera!

The reason I advocate analog photography is simple. That's where my heart is. I love every aspect of it. I am fascinated by the magic of light hitting the emulsion and stimulating the chemicals to create an image which is at that point still invisible. I truly love the process of deciding which film to use, shooting it and letting the folks from the lab do their thing and getting the images back. I marvel at the sensation of looking at a negative or a print. It is so different than looking at images on a screen! And I really worship at the altar of the giants who have come before us and on whose shoulders we stand today—They were analog shooters, each and every one of them! In moments of total delusions, I dream of becoming one of them. Take that, digital!

So, what does this book offer you?
This book drives stakes into the hearts of the myths surrounding the notion that digital photography is better. It revives your desire to enter the world of analog shooting and it helps you find your way through the various gates in the high walls around the realm of the un-dead. (Sorry for bringing back the metaphor. I couldn't help myself.)

Now I bid you, read on and enjoy „Film is un-dead! Five reasons why you should get (back) into film photography and how to truly enjoy the analog experience."

Five myths why digital is better than analog

The quality is higher with digital

Who are the top three photographers you really love? Whose photographs make you stop and stare? Which images take your breath away? Let me mention a few names. Are any of these on your heroes list? Ansel Adams, Annie Leibovitz, Dorothea Lang, Henry Cartier-Bresson, Richard Avedon, Michael Kenna, Ryan Muirehead (the list goes on)? They are all film shooters, all photographers producing images of the highest quality. Don't know any or some of the names? No problem, google them. You will be blown away by their work, I promise you!

Quality does not come from the camera but rather from the photographer. However if you just look at the technical side and take art and talent out of the equation, you will still be very hard pressed to find reasons why digital is better than analog.

Let's take on the notion that sensor size has anything to do with quality. In the world of digital, the object of desire is the full-frame sensor. That is supposedly the piece of technology that provides the biggest resolution, because it can gather the most information coming from the light passing through the lens. No objections here, but what does „full-frame" mean? It means „as big as a 35mm film frame." Now, compare the size of this full-frame sensor/35mm film negative (24x36mm) to the negative of a medium format film negative (60x60mm, 45x60mm, 60x70mm). Imagine the amount of information a negative of that size can store. And if you do a high-resolution scan, the file size will blow the tubes out of your computer—not literally, of course but beware. Those files are huge and beautiful.

How about grain, you ask? Grain is what you see when you look very closely at color (C41) or black and white negative film photos. It only appears when you blow photos up to a very large size. Then little spots appear. However, if you blow up digital images, you will also see pixilation. In digital speak: noise. So, no difference here! Noise as well as grain can get more pronounced if you use film with higher speeds. The grain is larger in those films. That is the trade off for using film, which allows you to shoot in lower light situations. Film speed is designated by the ISO-number. The higher the number, the more light it can gather, but also the bigger the grain. Digital cameras let you control the ISO as well; turning up the ISO can compensate for less light. If you do that, more noise will appear in your image.

It is a matter of taste, but most people—even the die hard digital photographers—will agree that grain can be very beautiful and noise just looks terrible. There must be a reason why there are so many apps as well as Lightroom and Photoshop pre-sets out there, which try to emulate film grain in digital photos.

But what if you want no grain at all? Try slide film (E6). Transparency film does not have any grain whatsoever.

Take that, digital sensor!

It is cheaper

One of the biggest misconceptions about analog photography is that it is more expensive than digital. Sure, every click of the shutter costs you money if you shoot film. There is the cost of the film itself, and you'll have to get it developed and maybe scanned. That all adds up. There is no denying the cost aspect. Analog photography is not free, but neither is digital. Let's do the math. If you buy a good DSLR, not the NFL-stuff, mind you, just something the average consumer would buy, maybe a Canon EOS 70d (which is, what I shoot, when I go digital for a project) or a Nikon D7100., you will spend about 1100 to 1200 US dollars. That includes the 18-55mm (f3.5-5.6) kit lens. The SD card you need costs an additional 30-40 bucks, depending on speed and storage capacity. Maybe you get a good deal and you score a camera, lens and SD-card for 1100 bucks. From there on your hobby is free, meaning no additional costs per photo(The only additional costs would be, if you want to make physical prints.)

Now go shop for a nice analog SLR. Not the old Minolta or Canon A1 your dad had when you were a kid. Let's buy something nice. Maybe a Nikon F100. You can get one from $150-300 with a kit lens, depending on the condition and your eBay luck. Let's go with the nicest one. So now you have spent $300. Maybe you want to show your analog photos on the Internet, then you'll need to buy a scanner. For $100 you'll be in the game. That leaves you with 700 bucks for film and development. You can get a pack of five rolls of Fuji Superia 200 for around $20. Each roll yields 36 exposures equaling 180 shots. Go double that amount to figure in the cost of developing those images in a lab. That brings us up to $40. That means you'll get 17 packs of five rolls for the $700 you have left after buying your lovely SLR. 17x5x36 equals 3060 photos. These are the shots you can take until you catch up with the price you'll have to pay for a good medium level DSLR. You can stretch that number by skimping on film. But that is mainly not a good idea. Good film is where a lot of the desired look of your images comes from. There are a few good and affordable options out there. Maybe you want to go for nice skin tones, then Kodak Portra will be a good choice. Black and white? Sure! Try Ilford's options. Another option to stretch your budget is to find a cheaper camera. The Minolta I frowned upon earlier can be had for about 50-60 bucks including a nice 50mm, f1.8 lens. The Minoltas are not sexy, but they are very fine cameras. They are build to last and the lenses are very cheap and of excellent quality. Do the math.

As I said, analog photography is not a cheap endeavor. Then again, digital is not cheaper. If you consider the typical buying habits of digital shooters, every 2-3 years the normal digital photographer buys a new camera body. In contrast, A F100 or a Minolta XG-M can live for decades and provide you with lots and lots of wonderful photos.

Digital is easier

„That's too complicated." These words are very common when you hear people talking about digital vs. analog. Now, let me ask you this: What are they talking about? Look at a standard SLR. There is a dial for shutter speed, one for aperture and you'll have to choose the speed of your film. That's all you'll have to think about besides focusing and composition. Now all that is left is to press the shutter button.
Many SLRs, especially from the 1980s, even give you automatic options such as aperture or shutter priority. That leaves you with choosing either the shutter speed or aperture setting and letting the camera calculate the rest.

Now look at the back of your digital camera. Even the most basic compacts offer a whole host of buttons, dials, knobs, menus and sub-menus. Just to mention a few: white balance, aspect ratio, fps, raw/jpg, bracketing... The list goes on and on. If you check the screen on your average DSLR you'll find a histogram, different auto focus and light metering modes. Throw in the question of whether you want your camera to beep when things are in focus, and you'll start to come to the conclusion that maybe digital is not easy at all. Sure, you can set your $1200 DSLR to auto mode. But then you can just go ahead and use your smart phone to take pictures.

None of the many digital functions I have just mentioned are useless. They are very cool options, especially for the advanced photographer. All I'm saying is: Digital ain't easy!

You can't buy film anymore

I was really looking forward to busting this myth. Why? I was itching to write this paragraph because it gives me the opportunity to quote President Obama. Here it goes: „Yes, we can!" Now please repeat after me, if you may, dear skeptic, „Yes, we can... still buy film!" True, many drugstores have stopped selling film. That is sad but not the end of the world or of anything else, really. Try amazon.com or www.bhphotovideo.com or any other online retailer. The offering of different film stock is plentiful. You'll find 35mm, 120 medium format, 4x5 sheet film as well as instant film. You have the choice between color negative (C41), slide film (E6) and black and white as well as some special films such as infrared.

If you want to shoot black and white and cannot find a place to develop the film, and do not want to do it yourself, there is the wonderful option of using Ilfords XP-2 film. It produces black and white images, but it can be developed in C41-chemistry. That makes it much easier to find a lab. Most drugstores still offer the service.

Film may not be everywhere like it used to be, but it is still easily available.

Film is for old people

Have you ever heard of Hipsters? Those cool young people who surf the trends of our times and are always at the forefront of what is in and out. Shooting film is defiantly hip, according to hipsters. Proof of this can be found at the unlikeliest of places. Urban Outfitters, the place that sells outrageously over-priced but very cool clothes to young people all over the world offers, alongside t-shirts and skinny pants, you guessed it: cameras and film!

The camera variety you'll find at this particular clothing store is what we call affectionately „toycamers." The camera maker and seller Lomography cooperates with Urban Outfitters. Those colorful plastic lensed cameras may look like toys from a Pixar movie, but they take film, produce real photos and are „way cool"! But we are getting way ahead of ourselves. We'll talk more about toycameras later in this book.

If you consult the Internet, you will find a large community of analog photo enthusiasts. There are countless blogs and websites, groups on Facebook and Flickr, and an entire social network dedicated to analog photography can be found at Lomography.com. Then there is an endless stream of video and audio podcasts on the subject. The Framed Network has even created an entire series of professionally produced shows on film photography. Many of the faces you see on the web, spreading the gospel of analog image making, are young.

Analog photography is definitely not just for old people who are stuck in the past, but neither is it only for the young and hip either! Many photographers who started in film and who have moved to digital are starting to find their way back. Often times they do not abandon the digital world completely, but rather add film to their toolbox. Those people who are sometimes referred to as hybrid shooters are probably in the majority. For most photographers it is not a question of film vs. sensor. It is more an exclamation of „give me both"!

Many digital cameras, from smartphones to DSLRs, offer filters that simulate the look of film. Instagram, Hipstamatic and other apps have picked up on the wonderful aesthetics of analog pictures. It is no surprise that many digital shooters, young and old, embrace the original, rather than mess with the digital copy. So digital is in part at fault for the resurrection of film.

Great reasons to get (back) into film

The look

Photos taken on film look different than digital images. There are numerous plug-ins for Adobe Lightroom and Photoshop as well as countless filters and pre-sets to emulate the very special appearance of analog pictures.

People just love the look! There are many reasons for it. Film images look different from the glossy and often sterile digital photographs we see every day. It is often quite hard to pinpoint what the difference is exactly, but it is there. Sometimes you feel it before you see it.

One of the things we have already talked about is the difference between grain and noise. The interesting thing about grain is that every film type has different grain. Ilford Delta film stock has very smooth almost invisible grain. Kodak tri-X, on the other hand, has very sharp grain. By looking at a tri-X photograph you cannot help but think of early street or documentary photography.

The color range is also quite unique to every type of film. While Fuji films have very vibrant colors which makes them wonderful for landscapes, Kodak Portra renders beautiful and natural skin tones, while otherwise being more subtle than Fuji.

If you want to go really crazy, you can shoot a roll of grainless slide film and have it processed in C41-chemicals, which are usually reserved for color negative films. This is called cross-processing (xPro) and makes the colors and contrasts go wild. No Instagram low-fi filter can come close to this amazing look. Slide film has become quite rare over the past couple of years. However Agfa CT Precisia and Fuji Velvia are still around and provide absolutely stunning xPro-results.

If you ask people to try to pinpoint what it is they like about film pictures (and digital pics that have been manipulated to look like film), the answers often stem from memories. For most of us, anyone over the age of 20 that is, we had our childhood and youth documented on film. The look of those precious memories is stored in our consciousness. Photographs of our first day of school and our prom were recorded via a light sensitive emulsion on celluloid. Wedding pictures, holiday snapshots, photographs of our family home and car...they were all captured by analog cameras. The look we remember from the „good old days" brings back warm and fuzzy feelings for most of us. Call it nostalgia, but it is a very real sensation.

I have already mentioned the notion of „just looking different." That argument is also very strongly in favor of analog images. We see millions of photographs every day. On billboards and in magazines, on computers, phones and tablet screens: edited to perfection or photoshopped to death, depending on your point of view, digital photos bombard us every second of the day. Now here comes along an analog image. It seems more quiet and subdued. You may call it „polite." It does not scream for your attention, it speaks softly. It does not sparkle in the same way its digital brothers do. It glows. You do not try to ignore it. You want to look at it, enjoy it and engage in a dialog with it.

A few months ago I wrote a blog post, which wasn't all that clever, but the headline really rang true. It said „love is analog."

The magic

Have you ever listened to someone talking about their Leica, their Polaroid SX-70 or even their Holga toycamera? Did you see the sparkle in their eyes? People fall in love with their analog cameras. They seem to have so much affection for these little light-tight boxes with a lens at the front. Sure, people like their digital cameras. They really enjoy bragging about the megapixel count and how cool this or that technical feature is—but they do not love their *mirrorless* or DSLR. Those cameras are „cool" and „the best," maybe they are even „professional." But they are never „lovely," „sexy" or „a trusted companion." The difference in love can also be witnessed in camera stores. People buy the newest and best thing their budget allows, only to come back in two or three years to buy the next model. Digitals seem to be more of an affair than a marriage. People stay true to their film cameras for years and years, often for life. Why is that? What is the secret behind this magic?

Analog cameras, especially anything older than the mid 1980s, are mainly mechanical objects. There really are no—or at the most very little—electronics involved. Things move: Sprockets move the film through the camera, springs fire the shutter, tiny curtains and mirrors do their thing in a very precise manner. Some genius has built the thing you hold in your hand. You may never be able to build such a complicated system yourself. But if you were to look inside your camera, you would understand what was going on or at least parts of it. Open up a digital camera and you would only see circuits and wires. All you see are dead and sterile objects that do not move. There is no way you could understand, what goes on in there! Even if you do not open your analog camera, you can actually feel the mirror move, or the advance mechanism drag the film from one side to the other. Analog cameras seem to be alive.

The medium of film is a thing of wonder and fascination in its own right. Think of the chemistry involved. Light hits a thin layer of emulsion. The light then sleeps in the dark until someone takes the film out of the camera, bathes it in developer, lets it swim in a stop bath before going on to the third potion: the fixer. Now water is used to wash the newly developed negative clean. All this takes place in complete darkness. After drying the negative you can hold it up to the light and you can get a faint hint of what your picture may look like. But still only a hint, mind you! In the case of black and white and color negative film you can only see a negative image on the transparent material. Now, still in total darkness, someone has to shine a light through the negative onto a piece of photographic paper for a very specific period of time. The paper—still white—is then put through three potions and then finally, you can see your final photograph. The process can only be described as alchemy. Chemicals, light and a bit of magic capture memories and let you look at them on a piece of paper.

Now compare that to digital. Light hits a sensor. The light is converted to zeros and ones. Then a small computer processes those digits and turns them into a visible picture on the back of your camera. That is truly impressive technology and I am very glad that it exists, but it ain't magic!

The element of surprise

Even if you know exactly what you are doing, even if you are a photographic wizard, you will still be surprised by the final images you get after developing your roll of film. At least that's what people tell me. And it is also my personal experience. We are so used to getting instant feedback from the screens on our cameras. We know immediately if we got the shot. There is no delayed gratification or uncertainty. In a split second you see the image. If you press the shutter of an analog camera, it clicks and that's it.

All you have is a mental image of what the picture might look like.

That imagined photo is closely related to the fresh memory of what you just saw through the viewfinder, But then you add a dose of speculation about the light, depth of field etc. You think you know what you've captured, but there is no way to be 100% sure. Experience and training do their part to give you confidence in your skills and the guessing game becomes easier, but it always remains a game, based on your speculations and assumptions.

The element of time also plays a role. From pressing the shutter to finishing the role of film, sending it to a lab and getting it back is such a long process that you are more often than not quite surprised by the photos you took. Who cannot remember the days when you picked up that envelope of holiday snapshots? You sit around a table with your family and start flipping through the prints, handing them around one by one. Sometimes this was weeks or even months after the pictures were taken. „Where was this? Did I take that photo?" Those words have never been uttered by a digital shooter.

If you want to take the element of surprise to a whole other level, join the cult of Lomographers. One of their ten golden rules is: „Don't think, just shoot." Another rule is: „You don't have to know beforehand what is in your picture." And the next rule adds: „...nor afterwards." This „shoot from the hip" mentality can lead to the most astonishing images and certainly to quite a lot of surprises.

The community

Analog photographers are nice people. They are more than willing to talk about their cameras and are usually very knowledgeable about them. They spend so much time with their apparatuses that they know them intimately. All the little quirks and capabilities have been explored and nothing gives the photographer more pleasure than to tell you stories of love and woe with regards to their cameras. There are an unbelievable number of places on the web where people share experiences, give tips and just talk about how wonderful their cameras are.

The same thing is true for the real world. If two analog shooters meet on the street, there is at least a nod of recognition, but more often, at least a few words are exchanged. „What have you got there? Ah, yes! What a beauty! What kind of film are you using?"

If you are lonely and are in the market for new friends, take a TLR (twin lens reflex camera) or a boxcamera, a Polaroid or a bright colorful toycamera out for a walk. You will definitely be smiled at and talked to. Try it! The encounters you will have are delightful. If you really want to stop traffic, I would recommend a Polaroid Land camera. The ones with the bellows that fold flat and use peal apart film or „pack film." I guarantee you, there will be people lining up to talk to you, ask questions and stare in wonder when you first pull out a paper tab, then drag out a black film sandwich from the side of your camera. Then after about 90 seconds you start pealing the two layers apart. Voila! There you have your picture in one hand and the paper negative in the other hand, both still wet and smelling of chemicals. Rubeus Hagrid would exclaim: „You are a wizard, Harry!"

So, if you are still with me and haven't gone out shooting with your digital camera, I guess you are interested in joining the community of analog shooters and want to get started. Here are a few suggestions on how to either test the waters or jump in head first.

Five ways to truly enjoy the analog experience

Discover pinhole photography

What is a camera really? It is basically nothing but a light-tight box. It has an opening in the front through which light can enter. In the back of that box there is some photosensitive material, either film or photographic paper.

The opening at the front of the box is usually a lens with a shutter. What the lens does is control the direction through which the light beams enter the box. The shutter mechanism controls the amount of light getting in. That sounds simple enough, but if you want to go even more low-fi, you can exchange the lens for just a tiny hole and use a piece of black masking tape as a shutter or a light tight flap or cap of some sort. The result is a pinhole camera or camera obscura, the most basic of all cameras.

You can buy pinhole cameras which are nicely designed and perfectly crafted for a lot of money or you can make one yourself for under $5. If you have ever taken a photography class in high school, you may have already built your own pinhole camera. Sometimes even kindergartens or grade schools dabble in the world of pinhole cameras, giving very young children their first taste of the wonders of photography. For them it must feel like magic rather than physics and chemistry. But as we have already said, that may happen to adults as well.

I suggest, you start building your own camera obscura before entertaining the thought of buying one. The money is much better spent on film or photographic paper. There are hundreds of tutorials on Youtube, which you can consult if you want to get into all the little tricks and finer points on your little DIY project. These tutorials are really informative and fun to watch. All you really need to know, though, are the following steps.

1. Find a box. A shoe box will do just fine. You can also use a cookie can or a lunch box, anything really. The only important thing is that the box can be sealed completely from light coming in from the outside.
2. Paint the inside of the box flat black. Spray cans work best, but you can also use a paintbrush.
3. Cut or drill a hole about 1 inch in diameter into the front of the box. You do not have to be precise.
4. Take a soda can and cut out a piece of the aluminums which is a little bigger than the hole you just cut into your box—a pair of scissors usually works just fine.
5. Flatten the aluminum.
6. Take the thinnest sewing pin you can find and push the blunt end into the eraser of a pencil.
7. Use the pencil-needle „contraption" as a drill. Place the tip of the needle on the aluminum foil and slowly and carefully start spinning the

pencil. Apply very little pressure. Let the needle slowly work its way through the aluminum.

8. Take very fine sanding paper and file away any edges and loose pieces of metal around the pinhole you have just drilled. Sand the pinhole on both sides of the foil.

9. Stick the aluminum foil to the inside of the hole you have cut into the front of the box. Use black tape to make sure there are no light leaks around the metal. Use as much tape as needed; it does not have to look nice.

10. Put a piece of black tape over the pinhole from the outside.

11. Stick a piece of photographic paper or film on to the back wall of the box.

12. Seal the box by closing the lid and taping it shut with black tape.

That is all there is to it. Your first pinhole camera is ready for use. Sure you can always improve the design, be more precise when it comes to drilling the actual pinhole or you can experiment with building a film advance system so you can take multiple shots. But for now your personal camera obscura is ready to be tested.

First, you have to find an interesting object or landscape to take a picture of. Some of the coolest places to shoot are those with moving water or areas where lots of people move around. Because of the small aperture of the pinhole you will require long exposure times to get enough light onto the film or paper in the back of your camera. Movements will subsequently blur. Running water turns into a silvery haze. People become blurred or will disappear entirely from the photograph, if they move fast enough!

Second, you need to find a nice flat surface to set your camera on. You will want to avoid camera shake.

Now comes the complicated part. You will have to guess the correct exposure time. This depends on three variables. Available light, the diameter of the pinhole (aperture) and the sensitivity (speed) of your photo paper or film. You know the speed of the paper/film because that is stated on the package jt came in. The pinhole size has to be guessed. If you use a very fine needle, the aperture will be between f150 and f200. If that is too much guessing for you, you can actually scan the hole into your computer, zoom in to 100 percent and then measure the diameter in Photoshop. That is too technical, though, for this first camera—"trial and error" is an important part of the pinhole experience.

Now lets go digital for a second. Yes, I said digital, which means cheating. But that is fine. You are the one making the rules, so you can break them anytime you wish. Download an app to your smartphone. There are many free and cheap ones out there. I use PinholeMeter or Pinhole Assist on my iPhone, both do the job. You can enter the aperture and ISO number of your film or paper. Then you aim the camera of your phone at the scene you want to capture and the app automatically suggests the appropriate exposure time.

Open the pinhole by removing the strip of black tape and wait until the exposure time is over. Put the tape back on and: Yeah, you have just taken a photograph with nothing but a box with a hole in it.

To remove the film or paper you need a dark room or a changing bag. If you use film you need complete darkness to take it out of the box. If you use paper, subdued light is enough. Just draw the curtains and turn the lights off.

You can take care of the film developing yourself or let a lab handle it. Paper can be scanned directly without developing it first. You will have to be quick and careful, though. You can only scan the paper once. Because the light of the scanner will expose the paper completely and almost turn it black. So do not pre-scan it. Just run the scanner once. Scan at a high dpi-setting for the best result.

Now you have the picture on your computer screen. All you have to do is invert it. The original picture will be reversed. This means blacks will be shown white and vice versa.

If you have a dark room set-up you can of course still develop the photo paper in chemicals. This lets you keep the paper, which you can scan later, if you like. The previous process of scanning directly, destroys the photo paper, but it is much easier. So it depends on your set-up.

Look at your picture. Is it too dark or too light? That means you will have to either allow for a longer or shorter exposure the next time around. Is your image very fuzzy? If so, the solution can be to clean the edges of the pinhole even more. Cleaner and straighter the edges mean a clearer the picture.

Now, wash, rinse and repeat! Pinhole photography is a very slow process. It takes practice and patience. But after a while you will really enjoy it, and you will love the very special look of the photos. The hazy waters, the blurred movement of cars and people, the ultra wide angle and the almost infinite depth of field caused by the tiny aperture, make for truly unique photographs.

If you do not like the entire DIY route, you can take shortcuts. Premade pinholes can be bought. They are usually laser cut to precise measurements. That eliminates guessing the aperture. You can use any film camera that has a removable lens and a bulb-setting. All you will have to do is take off the lens and stick a piece of black cardboard over the opening of the camera body. In this cardboard you will have to cut a hole and tape the pre-made pinhole to it. This should ideally be done before taping the cardboard to the camera. That way you do not risk damaging your camera.

If you really do not like making things or are just not

very talented with scissors and tape, you can just buy a lens cap with an inbuilt pinhole. You can get those on Amazon and many other places online.

Yes, there are also pinhole lens caps for digital cameras. But do you really want to go that way?

Play with toycameras

If you want to stay low-fi but want to take it up a notch, you might enjoy playing around with toycameras. These cameras are made out of plastic, are cheaply made and sport a simple plastic meniscus lens. Toycameras usually have limited settings; there will likely be one to three aperture settings. They are usually designated for sunny, cloudy and partly cloudy conditions. Toycameras normally have just one shutter speed, between $1/50^{th}$ to $1/100^{th}$ of a second. Because of the poor quality and the wear and tear on the spring-loaded shutter, that speed can vary wildly. Some cameras have a bulb-mode for long exposures and focusing is done by turning the lens. A zone system helps you guess, but not more.

The most common toycameras are the Diana and Holga. The Diana was first produced in the 1960s by the Great Wall Plastic Factory in China, which was not a camera maker by any stretch of the imagination. Great Wall was a company cranking out cheap plastic toys and novelty items for trade shows and carnivals. The Diana was produced in huge numbers and sold around the world for about one dollar a piece. Nowadays you can find models from that era at yard sales and thrift stores very cheaply or online from $20-80. I suggest, you do not pay more than $30-40. These cameras are old, are made of plastic and have a simple spring as a shutter mechanism. So, you might buy a dud.

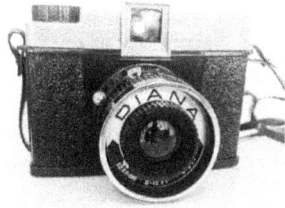

The Holga was produced in the 1980s in Hong Kong. It was meant to be sold in mainland China. The idea was to make a very cheap camera so everyone in China could buy one.

Both the Holga and the Diana use 120 medium format films and come with a very low-quality plastic lens. Therein lays the magic! The plastic lens 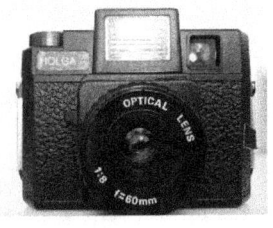 does everything you would normally try to avoid. It is not very sharp, and the sharpness varies from camera to camera. Some have a sharp spot in the center of the frame. Others are just blurry. Fans call that blurriness „dreamy." Reflections and refractions of the plastic cause strange color shifts and weird contrasts. You will also get vignettes, meaning darkening of the corners of the images. Adding to the „flaws" of the lens are the common light leaks, which occur because of the poor build of the camera body. Light creeps in through the seams of the plastic.

Dianas as well as the Holgas are both afflicted with these imperfections. The Holga is a bit sturdier than the Diana but otherwise they are true sisters.

Why, oh why would anyone want one of those crappy plastic cameras? Well, just look at the images. All the flaws add up to a very cool and truly artsy look. These plastic boxes with all their limitations are capable of creating stunning photographs. (With the assistance of a talented photographer, of course!) Go to flickr.com or lomography.com and you will be blown away by the beautiful images taken with the crappiest of cameras.

Vintage Dianas can be found in thrift stores, and flea markets. You can also get lucky on eBay. However there is always the risk that they don't work. The average Diana is 50 years old and made of plastic. So, sometimes you will be disappointed. Old Dianas are collectible, but please do not pay more than $30! If you want you can also buy a newly made Diana clone. Lomography makes and sells the Diana F+, which is also quite nice and actually comes with a pinhole option.

Holgas can also be bought used. Lomography sells new models as well, but you can cut costs by buying Holgas directly from the Holga Company. Even some camera stores like „B and H" in New York City sell new models at a much lower price than Lomography.

Besides the Big Two, the Holga and Diana, there is wide selection of toycameras to discover. Many of them use 35mm film, which is cheaper and easier to buy and get developed. There are crazy cameras with multiple lenses, so called „action samplers" and panorama cams as well as 35-mm Holga models. Toycam central is Lomography's online store as well as eBay.

Are you still not convinced that Toycameras are worth your while? Let me call upon a higher authority to bring you around.I have been granted the opportunity to speak with Sandra Carrion on the subject of Toycameras. Sandra is a photographer and photography teacher at Nassau Community College in New York. She served for 20 years as curator of the Krappy Kamera Competition and Exhibition at the SohoPhoto Gallery in New York City. Her work can be seen at

www.sandracarrion.com

Interview with Sandra Carrion

Q: *Sandra, you have run the Krappy Kamera Competition for twenty years. Can you tell me what that is all about?*

A: *Let me give you the history. I belong to the SohoPhoto Gallery in New York. It was in 1992. There was an opening and I was there with a few friends and we were looking at some pinhole pictures. And the conversation came around to the fact that I really love the quality and the simplicity and how honest these pictures are. And I really liked working with my toycameras, my junky cameras. We all started to laugh because we were all drinking wine and having a good time at the reception. And the three of us decided, this could be something we could do with the other artists at the gallery.*
Mind you, this kind of photography wasn't anything that was too well known at the time. At that time there was a little bit of a world there, but it wasn't really out in the open. So I put a note out to all the people in the gallery and asked them if they wanted to do this. And so we did this and called it Krappy Kamera.

Q: *Where did the „K"s come from?*

A: *I made it with the „K"s just because it made it look funnier.*

Q: *Is the term Krappy Kameras synonymous with toycameras or are we talking about different things?*

A: *No, it's the same. I think the King and the Queen of the toycameras are the Holga and the Diana. I think you have to define a Krappy Kamera as a camera that doesn't provide much assistance. You can't really control much of what's going on. You have to be really good to make it work, because the camera doesn't give you much help. You have to use all the tricks you have to make a beautiful image. Because what comes out of the camera, nine times out of ten, is not very beautiful.*

Q: *Were you planning on a long run or were you thinking: This is just going to be a one-off thing?*

A: *We began to do it annually for the people who are involved in the gallery. But then I was getting so many calls from other people outside the gallery that had heard about the show. So I finally put it out for everybody and turned it into a national competition. Then I started getting feedback from people in Europe, Canada and other countries and so we made it international. So, yes! Right from the start I knew this was something special.*

Q: *If someone had never seen a toycamera picture, how would you describe it? What makes them so different?*

A: *The idea we all have about photography is that we capture the world in a very realistic, perfect way with our, let me call them, „good cameras." You know, a regular DSLR or SLR.*
But there is a different characteristic that is inherent in

*something that has been done with an inferior lens. It's
something you can't really explain how it's done. It's the
imperfection of the plastic that does that. It records
somewhat of a reality. But there may be blurs or light
leaks or scratches or something on it that you wouldn't
allow to be in your regular or commercial photography.
So when people see these pictures they are always
intrigued. They are like: Wow! How is this done? I know
it's a photograph – but then what?*

Q: *I am very reluctant to use Photoshop on my
toycamera pictures because I have the feeling you
should trust the plastic lens and not to mess around
with it all that much. Is it ok to do digital post processing
or is that sacrilege?*

A: *I don't think that it's sacrilege. I think as
photographers you have to judge the image by the final
piece, by what it looks like. And if it looks like it needs
something else done to it, I think you should.
At Krappy Kamera the rules say that only the capture
has to be done with a plastic lens. And after that you
can do everything you want. It becomes very
experimental. People make tintypes, wet plates,
cyanotypes and large constructions printed on silk. They
do all these wonderful, wonderful things– but starting
with the image that was taken with this plastic lens.*

Q: *You work as a teacher in a community college in
Nassau County, NY. Do you use toycameras in class?
And what do your students say?*

A: *Yes, I'm teaching an experimental photography class which includes the krappy kamera unit. I teach photography majors. They are taking this class right before they graduate. They know the darkroom, they know the computer in and out and they know how to print. They really are very advanced students! When I give them this assignment and I tell them to go out with these toycameras they are stumped. They get very upset. It doesn't work! Then I ask: how many rolls of film did you shoot? Well, three. Then I say: after you've shot a hundred, you can come to talk to me.*

You have to figure it out. The ones that get it, eventually a light bulb goes off in their heads and they get really excited about it because it's so wonderful. The ones that don't get it are like: I'm never doing this again.

Q: *I may be crazy, but I have a feeling that my Holga speaks to me. Do you tell your students that they should listen to their toycameras?*

A: *Absolutely! You have to figure out what it is with this camera. What's going to make it happy? When it works for you it's going to work great. You'll see it in the pictures.*

If you want to take a closer look at a vintage Diana, go to my Youtube channel and check out my video on this wonderful piece of plastic.

A selection of Holga photos can be found here:

Go Lomo

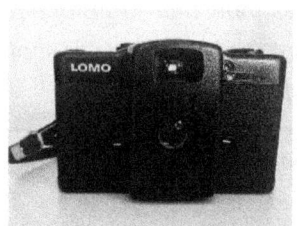

The term Lomography is derived from a small Russian camera called LC-A, which was built by the LOMO camera company in St. Petersburg, formally known as Leningrad. The Lomo Compact Automat was designed after the Japanese Cosina CX-2. It was introduced in 1984 and was made and sold until 2005. The small camera was discovered by a trio of Austrian students in a flea market in Prague just around the time the iron curtain came down. The three students Matthias Fiegl, Christoph Hofinger and Wolfgang Stranziger took their LC-A home to Vienna and played around with it. They quickly discovered that the images from the little compact camera looked different from those taken with other cameras. The Minitar-1 lens was quite unique. It did something to the colors and contrasts. There were also signs of vignettes and strange light reflexes going on. All this combined captured their interest. Add a bit of alcohol and serious partying into the equation and you'll get weird but very distinct snapshots.

Their friends started to take an interest to the quirky little camera and wanted one for themselves. Ever the industrious kind, the tree young Viennese men went all over to Russia and the countries of the crumbling East bloc in search of more Lomos in order to sell them in the West. The fan base of the LC-A grew constantly and quickly. Fiegl, Hofinger and Stranziger built a business and called it the Lomographic Society. The photos taken with the Lomos were dubbed „lomographs" and the lifestyle/art movement that ensued ended up being called Lomography.

As a guide to lomographers everywhere (and a clever marketing tool) the ten golden rules where declared.

The twin pillars of the movement are: 1) shooting fast without thinking, and 2) breaking photographic conventions.

Those rules still stand today and help you understand the ideas and aesthetic concepts behind Lomography. They make it very easy for newbies to enter the lomographic spheres. But let me warn you of the side effects: If the lomo-bug bites, it can change your life and take a big chunk out of your bank account. The cameras may be affordable, especially with a lively used market; however, the amount of film you burn through in your lomographic enthusiasm, can be quite substantial.

Rule 1: Take your camera everywhere you go

Rule 2: Use it any time – day and night

Rule 3: Lomography is not an interference in your life, but part of it

Rule 4: Try the shot from the hip

Rule 5: Approach the objects of your Lomographic desire as close as possible

Rule 6: Don't think

Rule 7: Be fast

Rule 8: You don't have to know beforehand what you captured on film

Rule 9: Afterwards either

Rule 10: Don't worry about any rules

Lomography may have started with the LOMO LC-A but it is not limited to this particular camera. You can use any cheap and simple camera you want. Following the golden rules and using cheap cameras are much more important. The toycameras mentioned in the previous chapter are very popular among lomographers. If you just want to try your luck and not jump in head first, there are other ways to start. You can just buy a disposable camera from the drugstore. You probably know them from weddings. The bonus: They come with film and are dirt cheap. Then there are plastic cameras with fix focus plastic lenses and just one shutter speed and aperture. Basically these cameras are disposables with the option of using them more than once. They can be picked up in thrift stores, flea markets as well as online. Do not pay more than $2-3! There are even panorama cameras available. Just look around! Armed with your budget cams, hit the streets of your neighborhood, forget anything you have ever learned about photography. Shoot from the hip, be fast, don't think… you see what I am getting at. Have fun!

(Re-)discover instant photography

If you fancy getting into instant photography you have three options. You can either get an old Polaroid camera, a newer model from the Fuji Instax series or Lomo Instant, which is offered by the folks at Lomography. Fuji and Lomocameras use Instax film stock, which comes in two sizes: wide and mini. If you decide on a Polaroid camera you can get film for the three camera types. The Impossible Project has re-engineered film for the SX-70 and 600-Line of vintage Polaroid cameras. The older Polaroid Land Automatic cameras use pack film (otherwise known as peal-apart film). Fuji currently offers two types of color pack film (FP 100c Professional and FP100c Silk) and the recently discontinued FP-3000b black and white peal-apart can still be found online. However it is running out quickly and prices are rising.

The Impossible Project has bought the last factory of the bankrupt Polaroid empire in Enschede in the Netherlands. Literally in the last second, a bunch of instant photography fans swooped in and saved the factory and the machines therein from being demolished. The idea was to keep instant film alive. First of all the young company sold the old Polaroid stock and then turned to producing new film. Due to patent problems and because many of the suppliers of chemicals and components had gone under alongside the Polaroid company, the film had to be re-engineered from scratch. The owner of the Sofortbild-Shop—Berlins only store dedicated to instant photography—explained it to me like this. „Imagine you have a car. You need gasoline to run it, but gasoline is not available and none of the chemical components that you need to produce suitable fuel, can be bought. You'll have to create a new product which makes your car run." That is basically what the people in Enschede are doing. They keep improving their product, selling issue after issue of new and refined film. Each batch is better than the last. Mistakes happen and are being fixed. The team carries on and on, getting closer and closer to the goal of making new film for the old Polaroid cameras. The name of the company, „The Impossible Project," pays homage to the Scientist/Entrepreneur/Wizzard Edwin Land, who came up with the idea of producing an instant film and brought the idea to market, and in doing so, changed the landscape of photography forever. One of his famous sayings was: *„Don't do* *anything that someone else can do. Don't undertake a project unless it is manifestly important and nearly impossible."*

The Impossible film breathes new life into vintage Polaroid cameras that have been deemed dead and buried. The wonderful thing about 600 type and SX-70 type cameras is that they do not need batteries. Therefore there can be no corrosion. All you have to check when you find one somewhere is whether it is clean and if the mirror is not broken inside. Other than that, a fresh pack of film– which doubles as a power source with its included battery–brings your Polaroid camera back from the dead. Which reminds me of the un-dead metaphor which I buried at the beginning of the book.

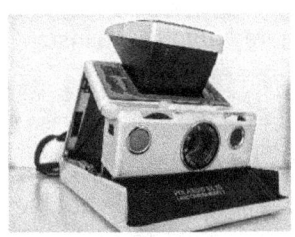

Impossible Film is quite expensive. A pack costs you about $20-25 for 8 photos. The cameras on the other hand can be found for $5-50. I have never paid more than 10 bucks for a 600type model. An SX-70 folding SLR can cost around $50-200 on eBay. I've found mine in a thrift store in Berlin for 39 Euros (44 USD) my second score was $25 Dollars at a flea market in New York.

Other Polaroid options are the Automatic Land Cameras. They are beautifully ugly. The come in grey plastic cases, sport a bellows system—and are so cool to use! The Fuji pack film takes some getting used to. However, once you get the hang of it, you are treated to a very special instant experience. Moreover, the image quality of the Fuji's film is absolutely stunning. Most Automatic cameras use mercury batteries, which are hard to find these days. The cameras can be easily converted to take ordinary batteries, however. There are lots and lots of videos on Youtube explaining the conversion for each different model. I converted mine to take two AA-batteries in 20 minutes.

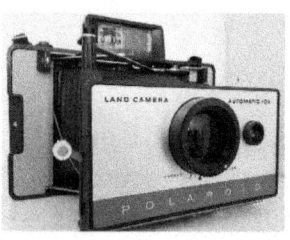

Fuji and Lomography are the only companies currently making new camera models. The Instax series is fun: The image quality of the Fuji stock is much truer to life than film made by Impossible, and it is much more affordable and widely available. A double pack of 20 shots can be bought for around 15 USD. However, the true (nostalgic) feeling, at least for me, is limited to shooting a vintage Polaroid camera. But if you look at the success of the Instax series there must be something to that format as well. As always, it comes down to taste.

Explore the wonders of the used market

The used market is full of bargains and treasures. So many photographers have abandoned film and moved to digital that the supply of used analog cameras is huge. Even though prices have risen in the past few years due to revived interest in film photography, even pro-level cameras can be bought for a fraction of what their digital counterparts cost.

Thrift stores, flea markets, eBay and garage sales are usually the best places to find what you are looking for. If a camera catches your eye and the price is to your liking, you'll have to do a few checks before you actually hand over your money. Here is a list of the Top 5 things to check before buying.

1. Is the camera clean?
Look at it from all sides, smell it. If it smells moldy or if it's really dirty, do not buy it.

2. Is the lens clear?
Look closely at the glass. If you see scratches or spots on the lens, do not buy it.

3. Is the battery compartment free of corrosion?
Old batteries can leak and cause nasty corrosion of the contacts and wires. If the contacts are not clean and shiny, do not buy the camera.

4.   Test the mechanics.

Test the aperture setting while looking into the lens. Do the blades move smoothly? Good sign! Trip the shutter. Repeat at the various speeds. Does every thing work? Look into the lens while doing so. You should see how the shutter opens and closes. Especially at slow speeds you should easily see if everything works. If you are looking at an SLR, remove the lens and press the shutter. Does the mirror move smoothly? Open the film compartment and press the shutter. Do the curtains and blades move?

5.   Check the film type.

Only buy 35mm or 120 medium format cameras. Those are the only formats still widely available. 110 films are still sold by Lomography, but this is a niche product and therefore expensive and hard to develop. If you stick to the before mentioned formats you'll be fine. Beware of cameras using 127 format. They are quite common on the used market. Especially the Kodak Brownie has to be mentioned at this point because there are still millions of them out there. They use 127 film which cannot be bought anymore. There are workarounds if you really want to go that way, but for your first film camera purchase on the used market, avoid them. If you are unsure as to which film a camera uses, check online.

Just google the camera and the film type usually pops right up.

Fun photography project to get you going

It is always good to have someone point the way if you are just beginning a journey. If you let me be your compass for the first step of your trip, I would be honored. To get you in the mood for analog photography, I would like to suggest a handful of exercises/projects. If you are already on your way out the door, do not let me stop you. You can just skip this part or maybe come back to it on one of those days, when inspirations seems to fail you and you need a little kick in the film compartment to get you shooting again.

Cheap camera challenge

Set yourself a limit of 5-10 bucks and comb your city or town for the weirdest, crappiest camera you can find. Buy a roll of film and go take photographs. Consider the limitations of the camera and try to find ways to work around them. You will be surprised how this simple exercise can get your creative juices flowing.

10 Friends

Portrait photography is a wonderful field in which the artist can really blossom. Where are you going to find models, though, when you are just starting out? The answer is quite simple. Ask your friends if they would like to be part of a project. Here's the deal: They show you their favorite place to hang out in their free time, and you photograph them in this environment. Limit yourself to ten people in order to keep the project from either being too small for you to build up a decent body of work, but also from becoming so big, that you will never finish it. Ten seems to be a good number for a project like this. Shoot one role of film per person. It cuts down on the costs and also forces you to think about each shot, before you take it.

After you have taken all these portraits, curate your work. Find one photograph per person, which you really like, and have the lab print them in a nice big format. Hang the photographs on the wall of your living room. Invite your 10 friends over to your house, offer a few refreshments and let everyone wander around to look at the photographs. Inevitably you'll get a ton of compliments. Apart from the praises and accolades, though, it is generally a recipe for a really good party with ten of your best friends. A project like this helps you develop a special set of skills, which go further than just how to shoot good portraits. You will also learn how to interact with the subjects in front of your lens. And, it will also be a great experience for you and your friends!

Filmswaps

Find a friend who is also a film shooter and ask him or her to be part of a shared project. Each one of you shoots a roll of film, then rewinds it to the point where the tab is still hanging out of the cartridge. Then hand the film to your friend; you will get theirs. Now load the film, which has already been exposed into your camera and go shoot as if it was a fresh roll of film. Get the film developed and marvel at the wild photographs you have created together. You will have a set of images that are made of two overlaying pictures. Some of the photos will be „unreadable" and terrible. But a few will be really awesome. Imagine your friend were from another city or even a different country! You could get Japanese street signs overlaid with your mother's cat. Filmswaps are very popular among the Lomography crowd. You will certainly find someone online who will be willing to swap film with you. Lomography.com or Facebook and Flickr are great places to find photography friends from around the world.

Environmental still lifes

Take two to three random objects from your house, stick them in your camera bag and hit the streets. Now, find interesting places and backgrounds and set up these objects. Try to find different ways to shoot them. I once spent an entire afternoon walking through the Norwegian capitol, Oslo photographing three apples I bought at a supermarket. This is an exercise you can also do with a digital camera, but I promise you, you will dive deeper into the challenge if you shoot film. Just because the number of shots per roll of film are limited, you really start to get picky about the places you set up your still lifes, the lighting and the angle you choose to shoot from. You can really get lost in your creativity and will certainly come home with a great set of images.

Black and white month

We see the world in color. Often those colors are so distracting that we do not see shapes and patterns. The quality of our compositions can suffer from the distracting stimuli bright colors can provide. In order to improve our sense of composition it is advised to limit yourself, for an extended period of time—say a month, to black and white film stock. After awhile, patterns, shapes, shadows and bright spots become much more visible to you. You start seeing the world differently. Geometry becomes much more important to your photographic eye. After you do this for a while, your composition will improve drastically. Even your color work will benefit from this exercise.

Great places to go for facts, inspiration and film photography fun

There are many places you can go to boost your creativity, find help and enjoy the growing community of film shooters. Here are a few places to start your digital journey into analog photography. These are places I go and enjoy immensely. I am not paid to send you there. I just think, you should check these places and people out, of course only after looking at my own website and Youtube channel. That goes without saying... remember the URL? No? Well here it is again: www.d18-foto.com

Camerapedia

Like it's big brother (or sister) Wikipedia, Camerapedia is a great place to find information. The contributors have collected a shear endless amount of knowledge surrounding analog cameras, film stock and lenses. The site is especially helpful if you are out hunting for camera bargains on the used market. It is always good to check Camerapedia for details on your object of desire.

TheArtofPhotography.tv

This YouTube Channel with its accompanying website is a wonderful place to check out if you are looking for information about the giants of photography history and current trends. The channel is not exclusively dedicated to analog shooting, but it provides hours and hours of high quality video to watch if you really want to get deep into film photography. The channel is run by Ted Forbs from Texas. The Art of Photography covers among many things, artists profiles, tutorials on film development, shooting techniques, camera reviews and lots more. Ted also produces documentaries and is just a swell guy to watch. The Art of Photography can be found at on Youtube as well as on iTunes.

Pdexposures

Pdexposures is a network of four audio podcasts. Pdexposures, the mother ship and oldest of the four, is dedicated to everything related to film photography and is co-hosted by Simon Ponder and Nate Matos from the United States as well as Tony Gale from the UK. Their lively conversations about cameras, photographic style and their love for shooting film are always great fun to listen to; it is also a great place to find information as well as inspiration to go out and take pictures. One of their trademarks is the $20 camera challenge in which they call on their listeners to find a camera, a roll of film and have it developed–all for just twenty bucks.

The three sister podcasts—The Instant Show, Pinhole Podcast and Plastic Imagery—pick up the style of Pdexposure but have their own unique voice and style which is due to a great set of co-hosts from the US, Europe and Australia. All podcasts can be found on iTunes.

Simon Ponder, besides being on Pdexposures, is also running the Plastic Imagery Podcast and was kind enough to talk to me for this book.

Q: How did the Plastic Imagery Podcast get started? Give me a little bit of the backstory. How did the tree of you find each other?
A: Rob, who is on the show, and I we went to college together. I was taking a photography class and he handed me a Holga and said „Go, shoot with this." I started having fun with it but at first I was like „what is this ridiculous piece of plastic?" So, one day we were out shooting and we had this instant back for the Holga and we got some pretty good photos out of it. Rob knew I had taken a podcasting class and said he'd really wanted to do a podcast. So we decided to do one on these stupid little plastic cameras. That was seven years ago. We did that for a while. Then it all fell apart. We were just way too busy. But it always stayed in the back

of our minds. So, when Nate from Pdexposures asked me to help out, he knew I had this old podcast and he said: „You should really bring it back." That's what we did.

Q: How big do you think the toycamera niche is? Are we going to be extinct?
A: Well, kind of... But no, we will not be going extinct. A few years ago it was really trendy and hip to shoot with a Holga, but now it is back to where it was before it was trendy.

Q: What do you think is the next big thing in toycamera photography?
A: I think we'll see new cameras appearing. 3D printing has come quite a long way and there are already folks printing pinhole cameras. So, I guess toycameras will be next. It's not that big of a leap. I foresee some very interesting stuff coming our way.

Q: What kinds of toycamera do you shoot?
A: I mainly shoot with a Holga. I have got one original Diana and I have been playing around a lot with the Lomo Instant and I shoot a lot of Polaroid cameras. But I always come back to the Holga. I've got five of them including the wide pinhole camera.

The Film Show on the Framed Network

If you want to watch three of the coolest and most talented film photographers on the Internet go on exciting analog photo adventures, then tune in to the Framed Network's film show. Over the course of two seasons, film shooters Ryan Muirehead and Tanja Lippert as well as photographer/stylist Tia Reagan have explored the history of analog photography, tried out a myriad of different cameras, explained the art of lighting and composition and shot everything from portrait to fashion and weddings. The show is fast paced, funny, informative and a little anarchic. If you want to pick up tricks from professional photographers who still shoot film and want to be entertained, the Framed Network is the place to go.

Lomography

Even though Lomo-Communuity has Toycameras as well as the Russian compact camera LOMO LC-A at it's heart, www.lomography.com has become a lively online community for analog shooters of every walk of life. The platform offers an online magazine which features tips and tricks, camera reviews as well as enchanting tales of analog adventures. Users can create their own Lomo-

Homes and upload their photographs, interact with one another and exchange inspiration and knowledge. The integrated online store offers a convenient way to buy film, cameras and accessories.

Now go and try it, shoot film!

Thank you for downloading this book and reading it! I hope you have found it valuable and entertaining. I shoot film and I really love to spread the word and hope to have inspired you to give analog photography a try. I wish you all the best with your photographic endeavors and welcome you to the community of the „un-dead." We are a fun group as you will soon find out. We are truly alive and kicking!

If you have any questions or comments, please find me at www.d18-foto.com, www.facebook.com/d18foto or follow me on Twitter @d18foto.

If you want to help spread the word of the wonders of film photography, please recommend my book to your friends and write a short review on Amazon.

Thanks and please come back to my little shelf in the Amazon.

About the Author

Dennis Eighteen is a part time photographer and writer, living in Berlin, Germany. He runs a YouTube channel and webpage on amateur photography, which can be found at www.d18-foto.com. He uses both analog as well as digital cameras. On his webpage he calls himself a „friend of digital and a lover of analog photography." Accordingly, most of his work is shot on film.

His camera collection ranges from Minolta SLRs to Agfa box cameras and from toycameras to professional medium format equipment. Twin-lens-reflex's, and compacts and vintage Polaroid cameras also fill his shelves.

Dennis spends many hours browsing flea markets, eBay and thrift stores. He is constantly on the lookout for interesting and often quirky vintage cameras. Unlike many collectors, he buys them to shoot, not to be admired on a shelf.

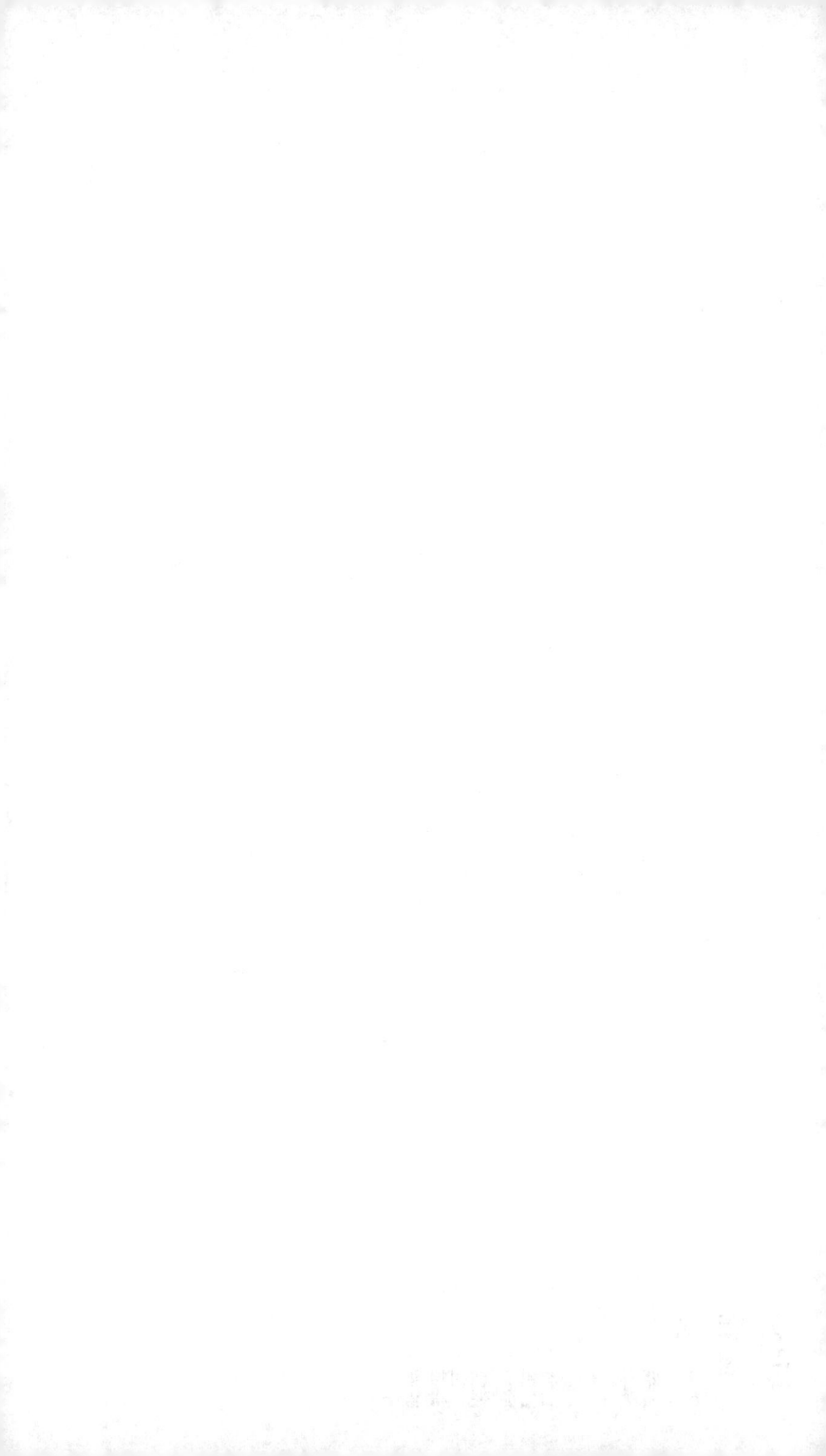